The Che

George (Soggy) Sanders

The Cherokee Origin Narrative

Authentic Text of William Eubanks' "Red Man's Origin"
with Notes and Illustrations

DONALD N. YATES

Cherokee Chapbooks

This text originally appeared in the newspaper *Indian Chieftain* (Vinita, Indian Territory) in 1896, reported by William Eubanks from the recitation by George Sahkiyah Sanders. Its title was *Red Man's Origin: The Legendary Story of His Rise and Fall, His Victories and Defeats and the Prophecy of His Future*. It was republished by Donald Panther-Yates with notes and an introduction, together with illustrations, in 2011. This is the fourth, revised and augmented edition, published in August 2017. It is available in audio versions and has been translated into Spanish, Italian and German.

ISBN: 197444161X
ISBN-13: 978-1974441617

DEDICATION

To the friends and descendants of the Cherokee
people everywhere

CONTENTS

ILLUSTRATIONS

INTRODUCTION

THERE are rare moments in our lives when we come upon an electrifying text. We have the feeling, "Here is what has been missing all along!" In the world of Native Americans, where oral communication takes the place of the written word, such an epiphany often occurs when we first hear—or first begin to fathom—the story of our people's origin, nature and character. In the past, such narratives were recounted in ceremonial recitations at gatherings to ensure their transmission to future generations. I recall a starry night in Tennessee many years ago when I heard the traditional story of the Cherokee people's origins from an elder. My emotions were mixed, ranging from "Why hadn't I heard this before?" (and being somewhat peeved) to a sublime sense of relief and resolution, gratification and gratitude. After that, my life was changed; it became more reflective, "figured out" and purposeful. I felt as though the ancestors had spoken to me.

Another instructive experience occurred when I came across a slim volume published by Bacone College's Indian University Press. It was titled *A Cherokee Vision of Eloh'*, edited by Howard L. Meredith and Virginia E. Milan, with Wesley Proctor, translator. Proctor translated the original English text into the Cherokee language. The tiny book that made such an enormous impact on me is hard to find today. So with the help of friends Richard Mack Bettis and Brian Wilkes, I have here transcribed and published the original English language text. It appeared in the *Indian Chieftain*, a Vinita, Oklahoma newspaper, in 1896, under the caption "Red Man's Origin."

We do not have anything "more original" than "Red Man's Origin"—not in fixed form. No version of the story has been recorded in Cherokee, only what was re-created from the English by Proctor many years later. "Red Man's Origin" is an English language newspaper article, simply that. We must be content with the form in which it survives, and with the fact that it does survive. It reproduces the words of George Sahkiyah ("Soggy") Sanders as translated by William Eubanks. Sanders was a fullblood who spoke little English and could only read and write in Cherokee. A friend of Sam Smith, he lived in the Saline District, where he became a senator. He also served as a member of the Cherokee Commission to the Dawes Commission. William Eubanks (1841-1921) was the son of a white adopted father and Cherokee mother. His Cherokee name was Unenudi. Acknowledged as one of the outstanding Cherokee intellectuals of the late nineteenth century, he used the pen-name Cornsilk in his newspaper articles, many of them of a political or anthropological cast. He was a member of the Keetoowah Priestly Society and a translator for the Cherokee Nation until it was dissolved in 1906.

I have made minimal editorial alterations in the spelling

and punctuation, and nothing has been left out of the original article by Cornsilk. Since this is our only testimony to Sanders' original Cherokee, the text is presented as closely as possible to the format in which it was published in 1896. A few explanatory notes have been provided. I thank Brian Wilkes for sharing interpretations of Cherokee words. For any mistakes, however, I bear full responsibility.

SO LET us now open our minds, eyes and ears to a precious fragment of the Cherokee national narrative about that people's past, present and future.

When we lived beyond the great waters

WHEN we lived beyond the great waters there were twelve clans belonging to the Cherokee tribe. And back in the old country in which we lived the country was subject to great floods. So in the course of time we held a council and decided to build a storehouse reaching to heaven. The Cherokees said that when the house was built and the floods came the tribe would just leave the earth and go to heaven. And we commenced to build the great structure, and when it was towering into one of the highest heavens the great powers destroyed the apex, cutting it down to about half of its height. But as the tribe was fully determined to build to heaven for safety they were not discouraged but commenced to repair the damage done by the gods. Finally they completed the lofty structure and considered themselves safe from the floods. But after it was completed the gods destroyed the high part, again, and when they determined to repair the damage they found that the language of the tribe was confused or destroyed.

ONE DAY while working, a builder sent me (Soggy) down to get some mortar, but instead of bringing mud I brought a board. So with the other workmen, they could not understand each other. Then the tribe held another council and concluded to move out of the floody country and hunt one more dry and suitable to their liking.

Instead of bringing mud I brought a board

SO THEY journeyed for many days and years and finally came to a country that had a good climate and suitable for raising corn and other plenty upon which the tribe subsisted. Other red tribes or clans to the Cherokee tribe began to come also from the old country. The emigration continued for many years, never knowing that they crossed the great waters. In due course of time the old pathway which had been traveled by the clans was cut by the submergence of a portion of the land into the deep sea. This path can be traced to this day by broken boulders. This was of no surprise to the clans as they were used to the workings of the floods.

Long years after they had settled in their new homes in the new country they began to hunt for the clans of the Cherokee tribe, and after a fruitless search for the others finally gave it up and established a new system of seven sacred clans to the tribe. From that day to this they have been searching for the five lost clans of the Cherokees. But after the search was given up they then permanently organized the seven clan system which were separately named after the principal seven stars in the Yohna constellation.

After this the Cherokees settled down and organized a government and a religious system of worship. This worship consisted principally of certain rites which were intended to teach the more intelligent the true nature of the heavenly bodies or powers and the laws by which they govern themselves and their younger brethren, the lower planets and their children, the sons of men.

After this was done and the tribe began to prosper in a more favorable climate and a richer soil where an abundance of corn was raised and game was plentiful, a new difficulty stared them in the face. A strange race of men crossed the great waters and landed warriors who began to attack the Cherokee tribe. The Cherokees called in all the clans and began to destroy the enemy. They used their war clubs with such vim that they defeated and annihilated the enemy with the exception of a few prisoners whom they saved. These prisoners were placed in the canoes and sent back across the water which they had previously crossed. They were told to report back to their own country what great warriors the Cherokees were.

Then in a few more years another fleet of warriors came across. The broad waters were literally black with the innumerable hosts armed with bows and arrows. They landed on the shore and begun murdering the Cherokees, but the tribe again called in the clans and began to defend themselves with their war clubs, slaughtering the foreigners by thousands, day and night, having given one another the sacred word that they would not eat or sleep until the last enemy was destroyed. They were again victorious and conquered the invaders.

*A strange race of warriors began to attack the
Cherokee tribe*

THE CHEROKEES then organized a little hell of their own, and having instructed the women and children to gather great quantities of pine resin they covered the feet of the prisoners with great balls of the resin and set fire to them and burned off the feet of the captives, and while still burning they placed them in their boats and canoes and were told to go home and report what great warriors the Cherokees were.

Then the Cherokee tribe became uneasy as most of the clans were a long ways from the scene of the great land of blood. So the warrior clans consulted the wise men of the tribe to see what the next move on the part of the enemy would be.

THESE seven wise men, one from each tribe, then called all the clans together and they then held a council of wisdom at the half sphere temple. The wise men ordered the seven clans to dance around the round or half sphere temple for seven days and nights. When the seven days' dance commenced the wise men entered the door of the temple, in which there was no light, as the light radiated and emanating from the wise men was sufficient to illumine the interior of the temple. At the close of the seven days' dance one of the wise men came out of the temple in the form of an eagle. This eagle formed seven gyrations as it ascended into the heavens. After the eagle had performed its seventh spiral evolution and disappeared into the seventh heaven, the clans broke up and went home, leaving the other six wise men in the dark temple, which was lit up by psychic or spiritual light only.

One of the wise men came out of temple in the form of an eagle

The wise men then came home and after consulting the e-ca-ca-te or Urim and Thummin told the people that these warriors would not come any more for seven years.

THEN the Cherokees trained their young men for war and all the clans were notified of the fact.

And when the warriors came again across the great waters they were fully prepared to meet them again. These warriors came by thousands and thousands but they had in the meantime, knowing also that they had to resort to some other scheme besides depending upon their war clubs, fell upon the idea of using poison in their wars with the terrible invader. They then sent some great warriors out to kill the great and terrible seven-rayed serpent and get its poison, which they did and placed the liquid poison in simblings.

AT THE CLOSE of the seven years the dark and terrible warriors crossed over like locusts for numbers, with boats and loaded with poison and arms, thousands upon thousands. When the enemy arrived the Cherokees and all their clans came in with their war clubs and the simblings filled with oo-ca-te-ne poison and running near the lines of the enemy they shook their gourds of poison and spilling the poison near them they kept on one after another, whooping as they went. The Cherokees cut at right angles to the first run and decoyed the enemy to follow. When the invader came to where the poison was spilled they fainted and fell down.

*Then they sent some great warriors out to kill the
great and terrible seven-rayed serpent*

The Cherokees then came up and slaughtered them by thousands and thousands. This defeat discouraged the dark invader and the war from that source ceased. The Cherokees then lived for ages in peace. And a knowledge of the war with the dark invader became in the course of time known only in story.

THEIR ancient worship of the wise ones of heaven was kept up. This worship was organized at a time that was beyond the memory of the wisest of the Cherokee tribe, and it was only reorganized in the new country as the ancient religion. The people lived for ages in peace and happiness.

AFTER thus living for ages in peace and prosperity the Cherokee tribe increased greatly in population. They built the *cah-ti-yis* throughout the seven-clanned nation organized on the broad principle of universal brotherhood, which included the whole world except the five lost clans. Then it happened, while the Cherokee tribe thus lived in their new country, that strange white canoes appeared on the broad expanse of the great waters. The clans gathered on the shore in wonder and astonishment at the arrival in their waters of these strange vessels. These white canoes hovered in sight for several days as though not confident that they would be received with welcome by the tribe. The clans, thinking they were beings from heaven, began to beckon to them to come to the shore. The clans also prepared corn in which was cooked sweet nuts, venison and other prepared food to be presented to these white beings in their white canoes.

Strange white canoes appeared on the broad expanse of the great waters

White being an emblem of purity with the Cherokees, they looked upon these white beings as a pure race from the upper world. The white beings of the white canoes were soon convinced that no harm was to be expected and they landed. The strangers were received with welcome by the tribe and food was brought in and given to them.

TOBACCO which had been purified and called the *chola* of peace was also brought, together with pipes, and the strangers were asked to smoke with the clans. Then the white strangers, which were supposed to be visitors from heaven and who were supposed to be such on account of their white skins, as the idea and emblem of white was purity and spirituality among the Cherokees, these strangers were taken to be such, asked that they be allowed a small piece of ground upon which to camp, cook and sleep; it was charitably granted. These strangers were entertained by the Cherokee clans very charitably and food and other articles of comfort freely given to them. Then these strangers made known their desire and willingness to remain with the native Cherokee clans if they were allowed to purchase a small piece of ground upon which to camp and sleep. They made known to the tribe that they only needed a small piece of land about the size of a bull hide. This modest request was freely granted to the strangers and sold to them for a trifling consideration. The supposed heavenly strangers then cut one of the ox hides which they had brought with them into a small string which they stretched around a square enclosing several hundred square yards.

The strangers were asked to smoke with the clans

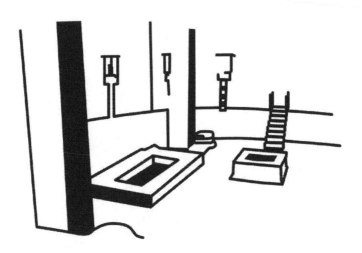

*All the clans gathered at the ancient site of the
sacred round or half sphere temple*

This they claimed to be in accordance with the purchase agreement to which the tribe finally agreed, saying at the same time that they had been deceived. Other purchases of land were made for which a consideration was always given by the white heavenly strangers, after the cession of which the tribe always acknowledged that they had been deceived. Then the tribe finally came to the conclusion that this white stranger was from the opposite pole of the heavens and put on his white skin for the purpose of deceiving. Then the Cherokee tribe began to destroy the white invader and as in the case of the dark invader they saved some to report what great warriors the Cherokees were. But the white invader began to use firearms against them and the Cherokee tribe was driven back farther and farther.

The Cherokee tribe then became discouraged and completely demoralized and said to the council of the clans that nothing could be done as the great serpents, the oo-ca-te-ni, had become extinct and there was no chance to obtain the terrible poison that had been so successfully used against the first invaders. So the wise men were consulted again, who ordered, as before, for the clans to hold a council second war dance around the round or half sphere temple. This notice was then made known to all the clans who gathered at the ancient site of the sacred round or half sphere temple. The clans gathered in except one or two who refused to come but when sent for finally came in. Then the seven days' dance commenced and completed, at the beginning of which seven days' dance the seven wise men of the clans entered the temple, which for ages had been neglected and only somewhat improved. The wise men after entering found that it could not be lighted with light that emanated from the spiritual light or from the wise men. Seeking the cause of the failure of the temple to light up, the lowest grade clan of the wise men, the terrible Sah-ho-ni clan, asked the next higher wise man of the second clan and he asked the third, and he asked the fourth, and he asked the fifth, and he asked the sixth, and he finally, the wisest of the wise, the Koola clan, answered and said: Our temple, ancient and sacred, has been neglected; the original fire, the eternal and primitive, has been allowed to become extinct by destroying the wise oo-ca-te-ni or the tanian, the wise of the tribe. He can never be found again until the other clans be found and the tribe reunites. We can do nothing, only to employ a substitute to illuminate our temple, and which shall be the outer body of the eternal fire. When the substitute for light, the fire, was kindled, the wise men looked upon their e-ca-ca-tis and could behold nothing in them but images as a brilliant light appeared in them originally.

The wisest of the wise men when he made his exit out of the round temple and began to perform his spiral evolutions in the heavens could ascend no higher than the regions of crude matter and after descending and reentering the temple so reported to the six other wise men. Then the wise men reported to their own clans, to the subordinate wise men of the clans, that the race of deceit and cunning had adopted a new scheme to deceive the Cherokee or red race.

Tanian, the wise of the tribe

THIS new scheme was the writing of a strange teaching that the white invader claimed to have been spoken from heaven, the truth or untruth of which the red tribe had to find out for themselves. We are still under the influence of this great monster and deceiver of nations. A tribute was placed upon the red race in land and gold to feed and keep alive this great deceiver conceived in hell and born on earth, and to remain under his influence to the close of the seventh period of the Sah-ho-ni clan when the red race will move from under his power.

When the race will, at that time, according to the oracle of the Stone of truth containing the image, be driven to the sea shore, where they will cross the water and landing in the old country from whence they came will find the five lost clans, become reunited into twelve clans, into one people again, will become a great nation known as the Esh-el-okee of the half sphere temple of light. They will become reunited into twelve clans, into one people again, and become a great nation.

The Phoenix

NOTES

1 **The first words** or *incipit* of the text in Cherokee would be: Dɓ ᏳᏓᏂᎥᏋ DᏠ ᏆWᎾ ᎡᎥᎮ ᏚᏕB ᎤᏢᏕᎶ. Transliterated: Asi tsidayotsehv ama tsutana egwoni duweye utliididla. Proctor adds the title "The Eloh" (i.e., old world), in Cherokee ᎡᎦᏗ Elohi. This land of the ancestors lay in the extreme west, like the Elysian Fields of the Greeks.

3 **Yohna constellation**. The Bear or Big Dipper.

6 **Half sphere temple**. In Cherokee, it is called *cahtiyis* (p. 10), which is Doric Greek for assembly hall. The same word was used of the Cherokee national capitol or townhouse. Henry George Liddell and Robert Scott, comp., *A Greek-English Lexicon* (Oxford: Clarendon Press, 1996) s.v. κάθημι 2.: "esp. of courts, councils, assemblies, etc. . . . of the βουλή." Brian Wilkes comments, "I think the word *cahtiyis* is a variant of *gatiyo*, which today means a stomp dance ground. Is the Stomp Dance ceremony with its spiraling movements a remnant of this older practice, originating in a domed structure and then moving outside?" He also writes, "I have been looking for a synonym to 'half-sphere temple of light' but find only meeting house, church, community hall. The word *tsunilawisdi* is used, loosely 'they assemble to meet'. Today, it's most commonly translated as 'church'. The related word *danilawiga* means a meeting for community purpose, and most commonly today is translated as 'prayer meeting' or

'church service'. *Adanelv* with the root *ada* for standing or tree/pillar is also used today to mean church."

8 *e-ca-ca-te* or **Urim and Thummin.** More properly, *igagadi*. Wilkes comments, "The 'gati' root refers to 'watch, look, calculate', and occurs in the nouns for a guardian, 'lookout', clerk, and others involved with calculation or assessment. If the stones were called *igagati*, this might by the equivalent of scry stone or keek-stone in English and Scots." Hebrew priests of the Temple in Jerusalem carried crystals about their necks called *urim* and *thummin* ("lights" and "protections"). Known as the Perfect Light, these crystals were carried in the breastplate of the high-priests. Cornelis van Dam, *The Urim and Thummin. A Means of Revelation in Ancient Israel* (Winona Lake: Eisenbrauns, 1997). Elsewhere, the Cherokee use the term *oolungtsata*. At the New Moon festival, if the High Priest or Uku saw the supplicant's figure upright in the crystal they would live. If the shape was cloudy, they may fall sick, if broken, they may be injured, and if prostate, they would die in the course of the new year. The alternative name of the divining crystal seems to be Ionic Greek, from the aorist participle for the verb ουλω "to be well," used in the same sense as the Latin salutation *salve*. **simblings**. Archaic spelling for simlin, cimbeline, squash, gourd or pumpkin shell. **oo-ca-te-ne.** Uktena. The name cannot be analyzed into Cherokee elements—a failing which often suggests foreign roots. It probably derives from *ou* "not" and *ktennais* "slain." In technical terms, it is the aorist participial form of Greek *kteino* "kill, slay." On Uktena, see James Mooney, *Myths of the Cherokee and Sacred*

Formulas of the Cherokees (Nashville: Cherokee Heritage, 1982), pp. 541, 297-298. On κτέvvαις see Liddell and Scott, s. v. The literal meaning is Unslayable One.

10 **cah-ti-yis**. See note for p. 6. The Doric Greek architecture of the *tholos* seems pertinent here. In its classic shape, the *tholos* consisted of a circular drum of columns covered by a parasol-shaped roof supported by internal wooden posts. The form also appears in tombs and is notable in the monumental national architecture of Washington, D.C. These public buildings in the ancient world were often constructed in a circular shape to emphasize egalitarian principles. The assembled citizenry, arranged by tribe and clan, sometimes reclined on bench-like couches or rafters as do many American Indians even today.

12 **chola of peace**. Tobacco is called the herb (*tsola*) of peace because it is used in the peace pipe ceremony. Other herbs (for instance, mullein) are also called *tsola*. Usage distinguishes between different applications of the same word, a frequent habit of Cherokee, which has a relatively small vocabulary. On ceremonial occasions, the Cherokee used "old" or "remade" or "sacred" tobacco, undoubtedly the case here. **bull hide**. Before coinage of currency (3rd cent. B.C.E.) ancient peoples either used barter or trade tokens, a standard type being the oxhide-shaped copper ingots or reel-shaped metal pieces of the Phoenicians. The point of the story seems to be that the white invaders offered the Indians money and inflated the value of it. The same story was told by the Phoenicians about their success in gaining the hinterlands of Carthage from the original native owners.

16 **terrible Sah-ho-ni clan.** By all accounts, the Panther or Blue Paint clan is almost extinct. It is also called Holly Clan, after the narcotic drink made from the yaupon holly plant or cussena. A famous member of old was Maj. George Lowrey, Jr., also known as Rising Fawn, Agin'-agi'li (1770-1852). He was Assistant Principal Chief of the Cherokee Nation and member of the Executive Council. He became a courier, banker, soldier, translator, law enforcement officer, planter, breeder and political leader. There is a painting of him attributed to George Catlin in the Gilcrease Museum in Tulsa. Sahoni Clan members were known as "Dangerous Men" and "Night People." Its Cherokee name Ani-Sahoni or Sakanike ("purple") means "They sit in the ashes until they turn blue-gray." Because West African medicine men are distinguished by white or blue face paint created from ashes, one might speculate that this minor clan could represent the African component in the Cherokee melting pot. Tribal traditions emphasize that the Cherokee include black people as well as white, red, and yellow. **Koola clan**. Kule, Acorn, Dove or Bird Clan. Much of Cherokee religion was under the control of the Bird Clan or the Ani-Tsiskwa. Before they were codified into seven, considered a sacred number by the Cherokee, there existed clans named raccoon, wildcat, fox, corn, water, Shawnee, crystal, wind, man, tree, tufted titmouse, raven, redbird, bluebird, holly, long prairie, blue, sun, fire, acorn and many, many others. Bird Clan people were considered good teachers, messengers and linguists. Its original name was Red Flicker, Sapsucker, Woodpecker or Ani-Tsaliena or Tsunilyana, meaning

Deaf Clan. Both the Wolf and Deer clans are offshoots of it. Its oldest name is Deaf Clan. Many chiefs, particularly peace chiefs, have been Bird. Chief John Ross (1790-1866, Cherokee name Cooweescoowee) was Bird Clan, descended in the strict female line from Ghi-goo-ie, wife of William Shorey, a Scotsman who became the official translator for Great Britain. Quatie Conrad was also Bird Clan; she married Alexander Brown, Archibald Fields and John Benge. Albert S. Gatschet (ca. 1900), Notes on Six Cherokee Gentes [card files in the Smithsonian Institution], including notations by James Mooney and J.N.B. Hewitt recording information from Cherokee medicine man John Ax among others, together with manuscript materials by J.T. Garrett, interpreted by John D. Strange, Allogan Slagle and Richard Mack Bettis.

tanian. Sea monster, Leviathan, Hebrew-Phoenician Tannin (T-N-Y-N), symbol of navigation and trade on the high seas. Curiously, Danauna was the name the Egyptians applied to the Greeks and other Sea Peoples. 18 **Esh-el-okee**. The original name of the Cherokee, not the same as Tsalagi, which, in the form *choloki*, according to anthropologists, designates "people of foreign speech." Raymond D. Fogelson in "Cherokee in the East," in *Handbook of North American Indian*, vol. 14, *Southeast* (Washington: Smithsonian), pp. 337-53, has a long discussion on *choloki* and its variants but reaches no conclusion. That's because Eshelokee is the name of the Tsalagi Warrior Society, pronounced Shalokee, with an *s* and *h*. The Warrior Society still flourishes in parts of Tennessee and North Carolina and distinguishes itself in this way from the overarching tribe, the Tsalagi, with its *ts* sound. Eshelokee specifically refers to the warrior caste and appears to be the same word as Greek *etheloikeoi*, "willing settlers, colonizers." On the prefix εθελο- "willing," Liddell and Scott, 479. On οικέω in the sense of "settle, colonize," s.v. A.2. Elsewhere, Eubanks (Cornsilk), writes, the Cherokees' true name, "has never been found out, and perhaps never will be," but it is a designation given to those "initiated as a tribe into the eastern mysteries . . . by a wise branch of the tribe known as those who spoke the language of Seg." He mentions the name "Esh-he-el-o-archie" and says that the Cherokee were instructed in keeping the sacred fire at "the seven Sacred Lakes." Seg is an Austronesian language of Indonesia, part of the very large family known as Central-Eastern-Malayo Polynesian, with a western form called Thai-Seg and eastern offshoot spoken in the Madang province of Papua New Guinea known as Sek, or Gedaged. There is also a tiny branch in South America. William Eubanks, "Cherokee Legend of the Son of Man . . . The Red Race, It is Claimed by this Writer, Were the Originators of the Ancient Apollo Worship, Now Known as the Christian Religion," in *A Collection of Works by William Eubanks*, ed. Doug Weatherly and Kristy Hales (American Native Press Archives and Sequoyah Research Center).

Tannin or Biblical Leviathan   (Tucson Artifacts 94.26.12)

BIBLIOGRAPHY

Adair, James (1930). *Adair's History of the American Indians*, ed. by Samuel Cole Williams, originally published London, 1775. Johnson City: Watauga.

Andersen, Johannes C. (1986). *Myths and Legends of the Polynesians*. Rutland: Tuttle.

Anderson, William L., Jane L. Brown and Anne F. Rogers (2010). *The Payne-Butrick Papers*. 6 vols. in 2. London: U of Nebraska P.

Bettis, R. Mack. Notes on six Cherokee gentes [card files in the Smithsonian Institution], by Albert S. Gatschet, including notations by James Mooney and J.N.B. Hewitt recording information from Cherokee medicine man John Ax among others, together with manuscript materials by J.T. Garrett, interpreted by John D. Strange, Allogan Slagle and Mack Bettis, and kindly shared with the author by the last named. Also to be thanked is Herman Viola, director of the Smithsonian's Anthropological Archives, who facilitated access of these materials in 1974.

Cherokee Nation of Oklahoma Cultural Resource Center, P.O. Box 948, Tahlequah, OK 74465.

Covey, Cyclone (1975). *Calalus: A Roman Jewish Colony in America from the Time of Charlemagne through Alfred the Great.* New York: Vantage.

Cunliffe, Richard John (1980). *A Lexicon of the Homeric Dialect.* Norman: U of Oklahoma P.

Durbin, Feeling (1975). *Cherokee-English Dictionary.* Ed. William Pulte. Tahlequah: Cherokee Nation of Oklahoma, 1975.

Eubanks, William (Cornsilk, ca. 1900). "Cherokee Legend of the Son of Man. The Red Race, It is Claimed by this Writer, Were the Originators of the Ancient Apollo Worship, Now Known as the Christian Religion," in *A Collection of Works by William Eubanks,* ed. Doug Weatherly and Kristy Hales. American Native Press Archives and Sequoyah Research Center. Published online: http://www.anpa.ualr.edu/.

Fell, Barry (1980). *Saga America.* New York: Times. See esp. "The Great Navigations," pp. 262-95.

Fogelson, Raymond D. (2003). "Cherokee in the East," in *Handbook of North American Indian,* vol. 14, *Southeast* (Washington: Smithsonian).

Gilbert, William Harlan (1925). "Eastern Cherokee Social Organization," in *Social Anthropology of Eastern American Indian Tribes,* ed. Fred Eggan. Chicago: Open Library.

Gilmore, E. L. (1986). *Cherokee Dictionary*. Tahlequah: Cherokee Studies Institute.

Hecht, Marjorie Mazel (1998). "The Decipherment and Discovery of a Voyage to America in 232 B.C.," *21ˢᵗ Century Science & Technology* 1998/1999:62-65.

Herm, Gerhard (1975). *The Phoenicians. The Purple Empire of the Ancient World*. New York: Morrow.

Jett, Stephen C. (2017). *Ancient Ocean Crossings. Reconsidering the Case for Contacts with the Pre-Columbian Americas*. Tuscaloosa: U of Alabama P.

------------------- (2007). "Pre-Columbian Transoceanic Contacts: The Context of Alleged Old World Inscriptions." *Epigraphic Society Occasional Papers* 25:13-17.

Jones, Terry L. et al. (2011). *Polynesians in America. Pre-Columbian Contacts with the New World*. Lanham: Altamira.

Liddell, Henry George and Robert Scott, comp. (1996). *A Greek-English Lexicon*. Oxford: Clarendon.

Mails, Thomas E. (1992). *The Cherokee People*. Tulsa: Council Oaks.

Meredith, Howard L. and Virginia E. Milan, ed. (n.d.). *Cherokee Vision of Eloh'*, trans. Wesley Proctor. Muskogee: Indian UP. Orig. pub. in *Indian Chieftain*,

1896.

Mooney, James (1975). *Historical Sketch of the Cherokee*, with a foreword by W.W. Keeler, intro. by Richard Mack Bettis. Chicago: Aldine.

------------------ (1982). *Myths of the Cherokee and Sacred Formulas of the Cherokees*. Nashville: Cherokee Heritage.

Oppenheimer, Stephen (2001). *Eden in the East*. London: Phoenix.

Pellech, Christine (2013). *Die Argonauten. Eine Weltkulturgeschichte des Altertums*. 3rd ed. Greiz: König.

------------------ (2011). *Die Odyssee. Eine antike Weltumsegelung*. 3rd extended and enlarged ed. Greiz: König..

Panther-Yates, Donald N. (2001). "A Portrait of Cherokee Chief Attakullakulla from the 1730s? A Discussion of William Verelst's 'Trustees of Georgia' Painting'," *Journal of Cherokee Studies* 22:4-20.

------------------ (2001). "Cherokee Story of the Sacred Dog of Monterey Mountain and the Great Flood: A Comparison of the Living Story with Mooney's Version," paper delivered at panel on "Storytelling and Contemporary Native American Culture," at the Southern States Communication Association National Conference Lexington, Ky., April 8, 2001.

------------------ (2013). "Cherokee Clans: An Informal History," *Ancient American* 15/90 (March 2011) 18-25. Print and ebook, Panther's Lodge, 2013. Audiobook narrated by Rich Crankshaw, 2013.

------------------ (2012). *Red Man's Origin. The Legendary Story of His Rise and Fall, His Victories and Defeats and the Prophecy of His Future.* New ed. of the Cherokee classic by William Eubanks, based on the original narrative as told by George Sanders. Cherokee Chapbooks. Phoenix: Panther's Lodge, 2012. Audiobook narrated by Shandon Loring, 2013. *El Origen del Hombre Rojo. La Historia Legendaria de Su Ascenso y Caida, Sus Victorias y Derrotas y la Profecia de Su Futuro* (Spanish version, ibid., 2013; audiobook narrated by Jorge Cisneros). *L'Origine dell'Uomo Rosso: La storia leggendaria della sua ascesa e della sua caduta, le sue vittorie e le sue sconfitte e la profezia del suo futuro,* trad. di Francesca Bortolaso (Italian version, ibid., 2014). Audiobook narrated in Italian by Cristian Vivi. *Die Abstammung der Cherokee-Indianer: Eine Spurensuche auf der Basis traditioneller Cherokee-Überlieferungen* (German version, translated with foreword by Christine Pellech, 2017).

Payne, John Howard (1832-38). Papers on the Cherokee (MSS and typescripts available on DVD). Newberry Library, Chicago, Ayer MS 698.

Royce, Charles C. (1975). *The Cherokee Nation of Indians.* Pref. by Herman J. Viola, intro. by Richard Mack Bettis. Chicago: Aldine.

Starr, Emmet (1921). *History of the Cherokee Indians.* Oklahoma City: Warden.

Strickland, Rennard (1975). *Fire and the Spirits. Cherokee Law from Clan to Court.* Norman: U of Oklahoma P.

Van Dam, Cornelis (1997). *The Urim and Thummin. A Means of Revelation in Ancient Israel.* Winona Lake: Eisenbrauns.

Wilkes, Brian with April Oliveros (2013). *Itse Yonega-Tsalagi Gasodoyasgi. The New English-Cherokee Dictionary.* 2nd ed. Tuscany Global.

------------------. Personal communications. 11 November 2005 *et seq.*

Yates, Donald N. (2010). "Anomalous Mitochondrial DNA Lineages in the Cherokee." *Ancient American* 14/86:28-32.

------------------ (2013). *Los Lunas Decalogue Stone: Eighth-century Hebrew Monument in New Mexico.* Phoenix: Panther's Lodge.

------------------ (2013). *Old Souls in a New World: The Secret History of the Cherokee Indians.* Phoenix: Panther's Lodge, 2013. Cherokee Chapbooks. Audiobook narrated by Rich Crankshaw, 2013.

------------------ (2012). *Old World Roots of the Cherokee.*

How DNA, Ancient Alphabets and Religion Explain the Origins of America's Largest Indian Nation. Introductory note by Cyclone Covey and foreword by Richard Mack Bettis. Jefferson: McFarland, 2012. Audiobook narrated by Jack Chekijian, 2013. Reviewed by James L. Guthrie and Stephen C. Jett, *Pre-Columbiana. A Journal of Long-Distance Contacts* 5/2-4 and 6/1 (2014), pp. 242-44.

------------------ (2017). *The Tucson Artifacts. An Album of Photography with Transcriptions and Translations of the Medieval Latin.* 2nd, corr. ed. Longmont: Panther's Lodge.

Yates, Donald N. and Teresa A. Yates (2014). *Cherokee DNA Studies: Real People Who Proved the Geneticists Wrong.* DNA Consultants Series on Consumer Genetics, 1. Phoenix: Panther's Lodge.

ABOUT THE AUTHOR

DONALD N. YATES, who has a Ph.D. in Classical Studies from the University of North Carolina at Chapel Hill, has written about genealogy, history and population genetics. He lives in Longmont, Colorado. For more information see www.donaldyates.com.

Made in the USA
Las Vegas, NV
04 January 2021